73

The Year of No Mistakes
a collection of poetry

 C3

by Cristin O'Keefe Aptowicz

Write Bloody Publishing
America's Independent Press

Austin, TX

WRITEBLOODY.COM

Aptowicz, Cristin O'Keefe.
1ˢᵗ edition.
ISBN: 978-1938912-34-4

Interior Layout by Lea C. Deschenes
Cover Designed by Chris Alurede
Author Photo by Jeffrey Paul Seasholtz
Proofread by Alex Kryger
Edited by Wess Mongo Jolley, Derrick Brown and Sarah Kay
Type set in Bergamo from www.theleagueofmoveabletype.com

This project is supported in part by an award from the National Endowment for the Arts. Art Works.

ART WORKS.
arts.gov

Many of the poems found in this book written during writing residencies granted by The University of Pennsylvania / Kelly Writers House and the Berkshire Taconic Community Foundation / Amy Clampitt House. The author is deeply grateful for their support.

Printed in Tennessee, USA

Write Bloody Publishing
Austin, TX
Support Independent Presses
writebloody.com

To contact the author, send an email to writebloody@gmail.com

MADE IN THE USA

THE YEAR OF NO MISTAKES

THE YEAR OF NO MISTAKES

I

II

III

IV

V

VI

VII

I

These United States

We met in Providence, Rhode Island, our country's
smallest state. Its motto is just one word: *Hope.*

At first, you lived in Chicago, where I'd visit and eat
breakfast out of a cast iron skillet every morning, and
I lived in New York City, where you'd eventually move
three weeks after the Towers were knocked down.

New York City was our base for eight years, where
the dotted lines of our travels originated and where
they ended: Austin, where our friends bribed us
with beer and queso; Charlotte, where the BBQ

was so good, we high-fived each other, our mouths
too full to form words; New Orleans, where our friends
married the day after you ate your first crawdaddy;
San Francisco, where we slept in a room with an iguana

and ate cheap burritos fat as puppies; Columbus, where
your brother lives; Florida, where your parents live; LA,
where we sat next to the hot tub our friends were in because
it never occurred to us to pack swimsuits in the winter.

In between it all, we lived in Astoria, Queens, sleeping on a bed
a friend of a friend was just going to throw out anyway,
commuting forty-five minutes on the subway each direction
just so that we'd have an excuse not to see anyone else

on the weekends. This is where we spent the earliest years
of *us*, where we built our first small home, crammed it
with all that laughter. When we finally left, our friends threw
us a party, and we smashed piñatas shaped like Death Stars.

Almost nine years earlier to the day, we rode through Canada on a Greyhound bus. We saw an entire flock of shooting stars through the scratched plexiglass windows, and made wishes. We were so new back then.

We couldn't see the mountains. We could only see the darkness where they blocked out the sky.

MANHATTAN

It was actually Woody Allen's New York City
that my boyfriend always wanted to live in,

and instead, I moved him into Queens.
I was as much Annie Hall as he was Alvy Singer,

which is to say not a lot, but maybe some,
maybe where it counts. The New York City

we lived in was not starkly black and white,
with a Gershwin score. We didn't

walk into delis with a dachshund named Waffles
or quip with Bella Abzug in MoMA's sculptural garden.

We never saw Truman Capote. Not even once.
Instead, we live in the present: a New York City

that even Woody Allen can't afford to live in. Or
maybe Woody Allen's New York City never existed.

It was the 70s version of streets paved with gold.
We fell for it. We fell for it every day:

skyline, lumpy as a nose, shiny as black-rimmed glasses;
the Yiddish we picked up through osmosis; character

actors at every turn: ditzy rockers, loud old women,
dapper old men, couples kissing hard on the sidewalk.

How can we leave it behind? And yet, we must.
Even Woody Allen knew sometimes you have

to leave her to create what you want to create,
on your terms. New York City has so many lovers,

but she marries no one. She strings us all along,
and my God, do we love her for it. How some days,

it feels like an old Woody Allen joke: *Such terrible food.*
Yes, and such small portions.

BROOKLYN

I don't know you at all, but
your women are pregnant.
Your pitbulls are hella nice,
and your small dogs are hella
arrogant. Hey, French Bulldog,
nobody gives a shit about you.
Stop acting like you're so
goddamn special just because
you are wearing a cool jacket.
Hey, Brooklyn, white people
are riding retro bikes all over
your face, and they are buying
coffees at prices that set a bad
precedent. Your granola is
organic and tasty. No lie. Brooklyn,
you are not Queens. Maybe you
never were. Maybe you and
Manhattan were always besties,
or frenemies, or wingmen.
You both get all the pretty girls.
You both get all the dreamers.
Brooklyn, I am from Queens.
I am not a pretty girl. I am not
a dreamer. I am trying to smile
at the lip-ringed barista while
straightening out the eight dollars
I need to buy coffee and yogurt
in your coffeehouses. I paw
the bottom of my purse for loose
change. Your borough's tween
girls look at me sadly. Brooklyn.
You make me feel old and poor.
Brooklyn, I don't forgive you.
Too many poets have written poems
about you, and now, I guess I'm one too.

Brooklyn, let's pretend we never met.
Then on our next date, I'll bring more
money. I won't stare at the women.
I won't try to pet your dogs.

THE BOWERY

We danced like ball bearings.
We laughed like ripped newspapers.
We smoked like backwards rain clouds.
We kissed like slammed doors.

We drank like taxi cabs in snowstorms.
We ate like honeybees swarming bears.
We screamed like willow trees in windstorms.
We wrote like a knife to our throat.

We fought like a thousand, tiny paper cuts.
We struggled like teeth against brick.
We fucked like rubber-necked car crashes.
We loved like we invented it.

THE BOWERY BEES

On the roof of the Bowery Poetry Club
are forty-five thousand bees. Like most
New Yorkers, the bees weren't born there.
The roof is empty and private and safe.

Like most New Yorkers, the bees work hard
to pay the rent. They make honey, two kinds:
Wild Honey and Orange Blossom.
It's for sale for $10 on the ground floor.

Like most New Yorkers, they are good
neighbors if you just leave them alone.
But sometimes, shit happens. The bees
have stung Bob, their landlord, the poet

who happens to own the club and its roof.
It didn't hurt, he says, and isn't it just like
a poet to see past the pain, all those barbed
stings meant to injure? And instead focus

on the honey, and the hum, and the hives,
soft living clouds of sound finding themselves
at home with the rest of us poets here
at the Bowery Poetry Club.

A Brief History
of the Bowery Poetry Club

At first the Bowery Poetry Club was just an idea, bubbling
under a porkpie hat. Bob Holman was a poet who wanted
a place for poetry to breathe and drink, a place to focus
all his own wild energy, an epic poem constantly
rewriting itself. There was a space on the Bowery,
an old framing shop, and soon it was ours. Or his. But ours.
Butcher block tables. The large gleaming coffee grinder
that was promptly stolen. The stage was constructed
so that it could be broken up and rebuilt and broken up
and rebuilt in any number of ways until it drove everyone
crazy, and so the stage became the stage. In the beginning,
there was the Walt Whitman illustrated in Lite Brite bulbs.
And after Walt, there was Edgar Allen Poe's raven,
harder to see: all black against an all black stage.
There was the café and its workers, the bar and its workers.
There were the sound guys who were all mean; different heights,
different weights, but who all wore similar ball caps. People
changed places. Jeremy the barista became Moonshine
the bartender who later became Mister Lower East Side.
Twice. Celena the poet became Black Cracker the DJ
became Ellison Glenn a young black guy who spends
most of the year in Europe. Bob became Hard-nosed Boss
became Ornery Over-seer became Good Old Bob became
Widower became World Traveler became Professor
became Archivist became The Man We Hug at the Bar.
We should always be telling him, *Welcome home,* but
instead we usually say, *I didn't know you'd be here.*
The café became another café became a juice place
became a snack bar became a café became a beefery
became an empty space. What will it be next: who knows?
Diane and Tanya were the O'Debra Twins, until they split.
Now they are just separate stars in the Lower East Side Art Star
universe, where they are joined by Zeroboy, a sound artist;
Mangina, an amputee; Juggernut, who plays electric guitar
with a live sparking tazer; a human carpet whose name

I forget; a famous novelist; and a sex columnist who wears
elf ears and has a Chihuahua she named after herself.
The Sunday Jazz sessions clashing with the alternarock
kids shows. The hip-hop shows and the poetry shows
which begin the same way: *So we are still waiting
for some people to show up but we'll be starting
in about five minutes. Tip your bartender.*
The drawing class you have to pay to attend,
where the models dress up as villains and the host
calls himself Dr. Sketchy. The comics, the burlesque
dancers, the performance artists who piss in buckets,
the puppets, the rock operas, and the puppet rock operas.
The $5 beers you'd buy for two dollars in any other city.
The cocktails named after poets: Pukowskis, Whitman's
Grasshopper, The Dylan Thomas. The sign we had up
for years which read: *Pretzels in the shape of Rods: $3.*
The babies crying at the bar. The drunks passed out
on the bench out front. The managers smoking pot
in the green room. The filthy couch that people kept
fucking on. Do you remember the lightweight tourist
who passed out in a basement bathroom stall and
how the staff never noticed, so he was locked
in the basement all night? Remember how he inspired
the rule: *Check the basement to make sure you don't
lock customers in basement.* I remember. I remember
the door fee I never had to pay, the doorman whose children
I danced with, the staff weddings which even to us seemed
like bad independent movies. Oh, Bowery. The last night
we spent in NYC as actual New Yorkers, we spent inside
of you. Everyone was there: the hustlers, the poets,
the bosses, the flirts, the moneyed, the poor, the hopeless,
the skirts, the creeps and the crushes, the drinkers, the dry,
the candy we bashed out of the piñata inside. The month after
we left, they installed two hives on the roof. Now there are bees
where once there was only a sky. These bees buzz and sting,
make honey to feed their beloved queen. These bees, they know:
sometimes you have to leave all that is comfortable, all that is
hum and crush, to do the job you need to do. But, baby,
those bees also know you never forget how to get back home.

ON WALKING IN NEW YORK CITY

From the apartment to the diner, the farmers market
to the bookstore. At the dog run, us laughing:
the sloppy golden stumbling around; elderly poodles
sniffing under the benches; the French bulldog
barreling like a chariot through the center of the sand.
Your hand finds its way to my shoulder by instinct.
We have been on this walk before. We have been
on so many: To Chinatown. To Little Italy.
To Central Park in deep winter. Through Astoria
and Brooklyn. Over bridges and beneath them.
To weddings. To readings. To dinner parties with
my parents. To the train station. To the grocery store.
To work. To work. To work. Through rainstorms.
Through snowstorms. Through the first year.
Through the tenth. Your hand on my back when
we cross the street. Your face on my shoulder.
How sometimes we don't know where we are going.
How we go nowhere and everywhere together.

II

SIMULACRUM

At the coffeehouse, I'm known as granola-and-yogurt.
At the supermarket, I'm known as large coffee, strong.
The old waiters in Queens called me *Christine* because
I couldn't correct them after nine years of mistakes.

To the first boy I ever kissed, I'm probably the girl
with a last name he can't remember. To the second boy
I ever kissed, I am likely the brunette friend of the blonde
he actually wanted to kiss. To my teachers, I was the front row,

the raised hand, the extra credit. To my poetry friends,
I am the deadline, the push on the shoulder. To my non-poetry
friends, I'm the poet. To my mom, I'm Cristin. To my dad,
I'm Pumpkin. To my nephews, I'm the person standing right

next to Uncle Shappy. I've answered to Professor Aptowicz,
to Ms. Cristin, to *Hey You!* I've been the new girl, the old
hand, the affable host. I've answered to a cleared throat,
to an awkward silence, to a snapped finger. This is all to say:

I wonder how you think of me now: am I still the crazy girl?
the loud one? the one who'd never go away? I know I was
the world's most transparent mystery, the persistent email,
the Christmas cookies you never wanted, hand-delivered.

If we met today, I hope I wouldn't be just an apology.
I hope I'd be the laugh in your fist, the second pancake,
the spilled coffee sipped from a saucer. I want to be that
great joke you accidentally forgot, the one that's still funny.

Shortly After Moving to Philadelphia for a Writing Residency, I Decide to Walk Home in a Goddamn Heat Wave

My sunglasses slide down my nose, a puddle
forming at the bridge. My t-shirt is now translucent,
the world's least-welcome wet t-shirt contest.

An afternoon of writing in a café and I am
cocky from the hours of air conditioning.
I decide to walk home. Why not?

On the bridge linking Center City to West,
I walk for seven minutes in uninterrupted sun.
The river is hot spit. A dead fish rides it upside

down, its shiny silver belly to the sky. I reach
the other side, but it's still ten blocks 'til home.
I am a dead fish, a cooked crab, a rotten apple

threatening to burst. I stumble in the door,
slick as a bathroom floor. My partner sits
in his underwear, fan blowing directly on him.

I drop my bag on the couch and head right
for the kitchen. *Well, that was stupid.* I say,
gulping tap water. He says, *I can't believe you*

left the house at all. My head under the faucet,
I nod. I didn't need him to tell me that. I know.
My forehead weeps pure regret.

The Waiting Room of the GYN

is always filled with babies and pregnant women.
This makes perfect sense, yet I forget every time.
It's like being in a renaissance painting: all stages
of fertility and life, and me, in my unwashed
pants trying to figure out the best way to say,
Please prescribe to me your cheapest birth control,
without sounding like the failure I sometimes
feel I am. In the private examination room, I begin
undressing before the nurse has even left.
Oh, and here's your privacy curtain, she says,
pulling it over to separate us without making
eye contact. Ten minutes later, the fingers
of a woman I just met reach around inside of me
as we both try to make small talk. *Everything
looks to be okay*, she says, with a snap of her glove.
Walking out, I always want to be given a hundred
high fives, this annual pilgrimage I loathe but make.
The babies tumble around the waiting room,
in carriages, on the floor, in impossibly large bellies.
One lady is breastfeeding when her baby pulls down
the blanket covering them. The woman's breast is round
and full, blue-veined and beautiful. She apologizes and
replaces it immediately. The women all shake their heads,
It's alright, honey, they say, *Don't worry. We are all women here.*

HOW WE DO

I tell my best friend, *See?*
This is proof of how close
friends we are,

that I am telling you
all this stuff in such
graphic detail!

And she said,
And my proof is
that I'm still listening!

MY TINY GOD

likes balance. He has me step in dog shit today
so I might catch an express train next week. He likes
how happy I am to earn it. How suffering to me is
like loading a gift card in karma's outlet mall.

My Tiny God knows I like established paths, following
dotted lines to my destination. My Tiny God thinks
no one learns anything that way, turns off the headlights
when we're still racing down a road.

Still, My Tiny God is the one I pray to on a rainy tarmac,
in the waiting room, on the other end of a static-filled line.
My Tiny God doesn't always take my calls. I don't know
if he listens to my voicemails. Sometimes he goes missing.

I remind myself he doesn't have to watch over me all the time.
He doesn't need to carry his scale everywhere. He is allowed
to get bored. He doesn't have to watch me write for me to know
that he likes it when I've written, to see the paper pile up.

These days, My Tiny God clocks in every morning. Coffee,
our favorite miracle. Work, our favorite song. Faith, our lucky
number. He pours sunlight on me like syrup, fluffs every cloud,
smacks the birds from the trees just so I can watch them scatter.

WEST PHILLY

I meet you here at the intersection of pitbull and
pigeon, at the valley of the screaming bus brakes,
where every thin squirrel and sweating toddler
packs its cheeks with leftover McDonalds. I meet
you where the sunbeams are filthy and relentless,
where graffiti washes its hair over train trestles,
its lousy dye job streaking everywhere, where
the bees come in two sizes: invisible and huge.
I meet you here where I first met you, last year
around this time, empty-backpacked and open-eyed.
West Philly, you are a cellphone shoved into a hijab.
You are a cop on a bike running me over on a sidewalk.
You are the same six homeless guys. West Philly,
I tried to love you, but you were smarter than that.
Knew I'd leave. You kept me at a distance. You
gave me opportunity and shitty diners and junkies
who hid stuff in our flower pots. You gave me time
and space and mouse shit on everything. You gave
me a tightrope, no umbrella, no net. West Philly, you
told me it's not that hard. The trick is to keep moving
forward, to never to look down, to never look back.

WHAT COULD GO WRONG

I.

We move back to New York City and neither of us
can find a job. It shames us, and we run through
our savings without telling anyone and it doesn't
help and we fight and break up, and that doesn't help,
and so we live on our friends' couches and take jobs
that pay nothing that we hate just to look ourselves
in the mirror and that doesn't help either. And we are
sobered now, waking up every morning knowing this
is the life we have earned, that this is the life we deserve.
The limitations so much closer than we realized, our faces
cracking against the glass of it. When our names are
mentioned, the smiles on our mothers' faces tighten.
They love us so much the disappointment keeps them up.
Where did we go wrong, they wonder. They can't see
how the flaws rose out of us like poison gas, how even
in phone calls we avoid eye contact, every word a fraud,
every silence a truth.

II.

Or we move to Austin, Texas, where all of our friends live,
and we find an apartment we think we can afford and
it is small and we fill it with too much stuff and we try
to make it. It is hot and things don't come as easily as
we had hoped: things like words, or jobs, or money.
Our friends shrink from us, stronger animals moving
from the weaker in the pack. They had such faith in us.
One day we wake up and we are broken. We taste it
in our morning kiss. Our mirror tells the same stories
in separate hours: things will never be the same. Years
later, we find we are happiest when shooting the chairs
out from under other would-be artists. We tell them
our story. Explain that what they think will happen

won't happen, doesn't happen, didn't happen to us.
We tell this story separately. We tell this story alone.
We tell this story to our mirrors, brush our teeth with it,
sing it in the shower. We tell this story every day.
It becomes the only truth we ever know.

An Unintentional Metaphor for What Happened Next

I searched the word *fireworks*
hoping to send you a picture
of the brightest, the most celebratory.

But instead, all of the images
that came up were photographs
of mangled hands.

Horrible Moving Tips
You Could Glean From My Most
Recent Move

Remove the grills of the toaster oven.
Fill it with your unopened pasta sauce jars.
Tape shut. Done.

Discover Christmas jar on top of fridge.
Open it to see if it is filled with old mint M&Ms.
Go to dump M&Ms out so that you can fill
the jar with ceramic dachshunds. Eat M&Ms.
Eat all the old M&Ms.

Find flat Christmas decorations everywhere.
Stick them on the side of transparent plastic bins.
Thus turning every bin into a Christmas bin
for no reason.

Know that you will feel better if you clear out
one section of the apartment entirely. Decide
to empty the entire closest on the living room floor.
Sit in the middle of the pile. Weep.

Decide to take a break just before you tape up
a box of your old college diaries. Decide
to crack open a diary for shits and giggles.
Hours pass in that black hole. Weep.

Decide to use up all the instant iced tea packages
so you don't need to pack them. Fill assortment
of water bottles while winging the measurements.
Some bottles taste like dirty water. Others,
like tea-flavored sludge. Mix up the decaf
with the full-strength. Drink too much. Weep.

Get into screaming match with boyfriend.
When he apologizes later, listen carefully as he says,
I'm sorry. But the heat makes me cranky. Wait a beat
before screaming back at him, *Well, it's a good thing
we are moving to TEXAS!*

Write a poem instead of packing. Look up.
Weep.

August 2011 Triptych

I am still up North, where the hotel room is so clean
and so white. I feel bad dragging an entire bus station
in with my suitcase. The crisp linens stare at me,
confused: my dirty toothbrush, my book bag,
my empty wallet. My heart is a radio interrupted
by the static of my anxiety. I have trouble keeping
a good connection. I spent all day trying not to think.
My heart is a radio that keeps jumping stations.
My heart is a radio I can't turn off.

You are in Austin, where you say your face
is a pizza, red and dripping with grease.
August, you say, is a great time to move there,
because it can't get any worse, right? You open
the door to our new apartment without me. I am
1300 miles away. The apartment is hot. And small.
And ours. The complex has a pool. There is a dog
walking around the pool that is not ours. There is
no *us* there. Yet. You turn on faucets, measure
wall space. This place will be a home, you say,
our home, a kiln where things that were soft
will harden.

Our future, I realize, is really my future and your future,
two dogs that walk next to each other, two leashes
held by the same hand. We used to be able to talk
about these dogs: what they looked like, how often
they needed to eat, if they were good with strangers.
Our year-long experiment of unleashing our dogs
to see where they would go has made them strangers
to us. We don't know where they go, or what happened
to them that they come home so ragged, so torn up.
Some nights they don't come home at all, and I picture
them in the street, hit and broken. But tonight, I hear
our futures whine and bark at separate doors. Tonight,
I hold my leash heavy in my hand. Tonight, the moon
is so bright I can't look at it.

III

AUSTIN

is a summer camp where it is always August.
The dogs bark steam here. There are no sidewalks.
Instead, there are whole football fields of yellow grass.
There are lizards who climb my apartment stairs.
Two nights ago, the Manhattan skyline spread her legs
for me one last time. Everything exploded with light. Jesus.
Now, the moon is a far-off smile. Trucks are like city buses
for one. I am called *Dear*. I am called *Sweetheart*.
The waitress asks if I want seconds. *Seconds are free,*
she adds. They know my number here. Yesterday,
I looked at our new apartment and told myself,
This is where I will write my next book. The apartment
stared back at me, confused. The news anchor tells me
it is our seventy-eighth consecutive 100+ degree day.
It is September. Somewhere, a maple leaf is changing color.
Somewhere a pumpkin scone is being baked. Somewhere
someone is putting their bathing suits into a box marked,
Summer. But here in Austin, my living room window is
an oven I can't shut off. Here, the sun is a fat loud bully
that everyone else has learned to like. Here, my afternoon walk
tried to kill me. In New York, the subway dives underground
without me. In New York, people are arguing about bagels.
In New York, a whole city wakes up to go to work.
I am in Austin now. I will still wake up. I will still go to work.
I will write the book. I will make a home.

THROUGH THE LOOKING GLASS

He calls me from the bus stop to tell me the job interview
was yet another scam. *When he described the job*, he tells me,
the guy literally drew a pyramid. The night before, we watched
the four-year-old daughter of a friend hide things in a tree.
She told us to close our eyes and when we did she'd yell,
Surprise! and show us the objects she'd stuffed into the tree.
Oh! we'd shout. *Where did they come from! Are you magic?*
She nodded and we all believed her. That night, he looked up
more job listings on Craigslist, more resumes, more calls,
more emails, more bills. This afternoon, he sweats in his suit
at the bus stop, his resumes wilt in their folder. *It's out there,*
he says, *there has got to be a job waiting for me out there,*
right?

THE ROAD MOST TRAVELED
NEVER LEFT QUEENS

On that road, I am the plumpest bride.
At the office, I polish my shiniest smile.

My clothes just want to become worn down,
so desperate they are to be unnoticed.

That road is lined with much richer people,
which is to say, it's in New York City.

The subway is a chariot I ride every day.
The chip on my shoulder is being pressed

into a diamond. My computer is a happy dog
I pet for hours, but who can do no tricks.

On that road, the apartment I left is still cheap,
is still mine. The ceiling, a road map I can't

decipher. The window, a radio I can't turn off.
The life I live now is that risk I didn't take.

I sleep every night in a warm bed, safe.
And when the alarm goes off, I wake up.

UNEMPLOYMENT

My boyfriend wakes up at noon, exhausted.

The day is a rainstorm he is forced to step into.

Life is a knife stuck in his bank account.

Lunch is the hour he worked sixteen months ago.

The mirror is a glass he is tilting

to see if he can collect enough

for one more swallow.

TRICKLE DOWN ECONOMICS

The dog has heartworm. The vet bill has
a lot of numbers. My body's largest organ
is its skin, and it won't stop being itchy,
being prickly, uncomfortably hot. *Money.*
My partner is unemployed, underemployed.
Two years now, and he's begun lying about
the bills he's paid because he *wants* to have
the money to pay them. He can't accept that
the money isn't there anymore. Two years,
and sometimes I go out to eat without him,
just so I can order whatever I want without
feeling guilty. *Money*, I tell him, *do you want
to break up over money?* No, of course not,
but here we are anyway: in the living room,
dog cringing on the couch as we scream
so loudly, the jar of loose change by the door
rattles like a snake preparing to strike.

IV

AUTOFILL

There are secrets
that only the search box
of my laptop knows.

Every Bad Thought

Sometimes I worry
that I'd like you better
if you just weren't
here.

Right There Yes

Some women fake their orgasms
to hear the sound of their own voices.
Ironically, it gets them off.

I, too, have written poems I wanted
to be true, but knew likely weren't.
Sometimes you want to say the spell,

hoping it is enough to cast it.

To Everyone Who Said
It Was Going to Be Okay

It wasn't,
but that's okay.

WHERE IT ENDS

On the couch, our hearts strained
against their cages. Our mouths.

THE TELLING

My mother says she'll tell my father
so I don't have to. I tell my brother
via email, so I get all the details right
without the words cracking in my throat.
My sister gets my brother's email, copy-
and-pasted with a foreword. My best friend
gets the phone call, her children screaming
in the next room. When I push the button
to hang up, I put the phone back to my ear
just to listen to the silence. They say
this generation will never know
the sound of a dial tone.

Summer Weather

Last night, the nervous weatherman warned
that there would be three days of thunderstorms.
When I looked out the window this morning,
I could see nothing but bright, blue sunshine.
I should probably write a poem about that, I thought,
before I left the house to not write anything at all.
It would be the week I told every member of my family
the news: that one half was now going to be my whole.
Eleven years, and we both let go at the same time.
Every morning now, I wake up and it is just me.
Every morning, my toothbrush is the only thing I kiss.
When I tell them, everyone hugs me, says they saw it coming.
When I finish, everyone predicts I will come out of this okay.
Afterwards I walk home alone through the summer heat,
the sunshine beating me so hard, my eyes can't stop sweating.

33 & 1/3

This morning, I wrote *LET IT GO* on my hand
in thick, black ink. I am thirty-three and I can't
believe I still have to do this. Driving to coffee,
the sky rips itself open, cries all over the place.
The cars slow and linger in it, headlights glow
and steam. When I finally arrive, the barista
sees the writing on my hand and says nothing.
But she gives me my change with two palms:
one reaching towards me from above, the other
holding me from below. I can't write poems
about you. It is impossible. A friend said when
she writes, her husband is a large grizzly bear,
her children are five tiny hearts in five lanterns,
and she is the little girl hiding a mermaid, or
the wife of a dog trained to walk on his back legs,
or the boy who orders a woman's heart for dinner
and gets it. *You don't always have to be so literal,*
she says. *That's why it's poetry.* But I can't help it.
I am always me. My hand is always my hand.
The black letters tell the story of my whole life
to anyone who wants to read it: *LET IT GO.*
This morning, the *it* was you.

Things that Happened During Petsitting that I Remind Myself Are Not Metaphors for My Heart

The dog refuses to eat. I keep filling her bowl
anyway: new kibble on top of old, hoping
that it will suddenly becoming tempting.

When I write, the cat watches me from a chair.
When I look at him, he purrs loudly, leans forward
so that I might touch him. I don't.

Now the dog refuses to come out of her cage,
no matter what I say, no matter how wide I open
the door. She knows that I am not her master.

On the couch, the cat crawls on top of me
and loves me so hard, his claws draw blood.
I am so lonely, I do nothing to stop it.

There are lights in this house I want to turn on,
but I can't find their switches. Outside, an engine
turns and turns in the night, but never catches.

CLEAVE

A relationship is not a thing; it is not
an achievement, we hear someone say
on TV two months after we finally said it
to each other: *Separation.* But

we can still be friends, right? And so
until the lease is up, I crawl next to you
into our old bed. Our feet are now strangers.
My body is my own again. Nobody sees it.

Sometimes, I fall into its arms to cry a bit.
It seems silly, to cry alone. I keep thinking
I should have better things to do. At night,
I tell the mirror it will be okay.

Great women have lived amazing lives *alone.*
Sometimes for a little while, sometimes forever.
I could be great, I keep telling the mirror,
if I could just get it together.

But my body doesn't listen. It keeps wanting.
Last night, I finally slept alone and woke to find
my body stretched parallel to the headboard.
Even in sleep, my body was searching,

rolling and turning in the empty sheets,
just wanting to be close to something.

Girls in Their Winter Dresses

There are women who men fall in love with,
I tell him, *and then there are the rest of us.*

Everyone knows what team we play for,
I continue, *and it's okay.* He shakes his head

at the idea, but can't verbalize why it's wrong.
And that's it. Which is to say, that is exactly it.

Every morning, I wake up in an empty bed.
I know what team I'm on. And it is okay.

I guess everyone feels this way after a break-up,
I say to no one.

But you know I love you, right?
no one says back.

What I Meant When I Said *Failure*

Friend sells two hundred dollars worth of chapbooks in 24 hours.
Friend fills entire performance hall for his book release.
Friend gets his residency paid for by online fundraiser.
Friend gets into every MFA program she applied to.

Friend gets seven Amazon reviews in less than a month.
Friend gets an invitation to open for my high school idol.
Friend gets prestigious award and is praised.
Friend gets flown around the world to read poetry.

Friend can't believe she's a size zero in this store!
Friend always packs a healthy meal to eat.
Friend makes yoga a priority, everyday, no matter what.
Friend just happened to be born rich.

Friend learned how to put on makeup as a teenager.
Friend seems to be having great sex all the time.
Friend demands everyone be silent and they are.
Friend is an adorable drunk.

Friend's mother thinks she is beautiful and perfect.
Friend's wedding was the very definition of love.
Friend's two dogs snore at the foot of her bed.
Friend's house looks like an actual adult lives there.

Op-Ed for The Sad Sack Review, Regarding News of Another Rash of Writer Suicides

In a fit of gloom, I googled the word *failure*,
just to see if my name would come up. Instead,
Google told me I misspelled the word *failure*.

Recounting this makes me feel like I'm starting
a very weepy poem, or a very dull suicide note.
Never begin a wedding toast with the dictionary

definition of *marriage*, and never begin a suicide
note by saying you googled the word *failure*.
These days, the number one thing preventing me

from killing myself is likely the idea of people
learning of my suicide via Facebook status updates.
There's no dignity in that eulogy, its collections

of sad face emoticons, studded with apostrophe tears.
This is a dumb reason to keep living, but it is a reason.
I'm sure all you other sad sacks have your reasons too.

So let's all cling to them. Let's all agree that living
for a dumb reason is better than killing yourself
for a dumb reason. Let's feed tears to the dragons

of misery, but let's never crawl into their mouths.
Let's write terrible poetry, dress like late-era Rothkos,
wear out the relentless hate machines of our brains,

but let's never break. Let's just keep living. We can
do this. Trust me. Yours Sincerely, Me, A Poet Who
Doesn't Even Know How to Spell the Word *Failure*.

Said the Fly Killing Itself Trying to Escape Through a Closed Window, Completely Ignoring the Open Door

Don't worry,
I'm not a metaphor.

WILD GEESE
after Mary Oliver

You don't have to be crushed
under the spokes of your own desire
to be proven worthy enough.

The trophies of your hard work
don't have to appear so freshly on your body.
Your clothes need not be torn.

Every night, you worry a new bird's nest
into your hair. Every night, your dreams
grind you under her boot heel.

Your pendulum heart doesn't need
to swing so hard in either direction.
Nails don't have to be bitten to the nub.

You have to believe that the ground will
materialize under your feet the moment
you step forward. No one can tell you

if it will be rock-gravel, or slick with pain.
No one can travel this road before you do.
It is yours, and it is beautiful because of it.

The Poets' Wedding in New Orleans

for Alexis and Anis

was held outdoors in a park in late May. We sat under the trees
and watched the pinwheels refuse to move, not even a hint
of a breeze. Soon humidity shoved its hands down our collars,
under our pant legs, dampened each wilting necktie. Make-up
slowly dissolved. Crew cuts shimmered with sweat. Even
the toddlers sat in the centers of hula hoops, and held leaves
to their cheeks. Young couples tried their best, kissing
with hot earnestness, until a defeated partner would say,
Okay, okay. That's enough. We waited. We didn't realize
the tartlets on the table were slowly cooking, egg cream
turning into omelet. We didn't know the frozen strawberries
being used as ice would give up so easily, breaking apart
in the lemonade like small, exploding hearts. What we did know
was that we stand when the bride arrives, all of us humming
Here Comes in the Bride into kazoos. She is, of course, beautiful:
flush with what we all know is love, floating towards her groom,
who grins like a happy bloodhound. They say every word just
to each other. She promises bike rides, adventure, teamwork.
He promises something so quiet we can't hear it, his hands
fluttering like nervous sparrows over his excited heart.
The minister finally says it, and it is done. They are married.
And when they kiss, we clap our palms to our chests and scream.
They run down the aisle, hand-in-hand, burst into the sunlight.
They don't stop, they keep running, laughing, eyes locked forward
to that bright future. Not even the wind tries to stop them.

JUNE

It had just turned summer in Texas when I became
no one's sweetheart.

I put lonesome on like an old coat, found things
I left in its pockets. *Winter*, I say. *I remember this.*

All summer long, I live behind a door.
On the other side of the door is everything.

It is June now. It is winter all the time.
But when I think of you, I light up like Christmas.

YOUR FRIENDS ARE HAVING MORE SEX THAN YOU

and they are having better sex too. They are making more money at their jobs, which are more fulfilling. They have better-looking co-workers, who laugh at their jokes. Your friends are reading books that will improve their lives, making them smarter, kinder, making them look better naked. Your friends don't need as much sleep as you. Thanks to their new diet they have so much more energy. Your friends not only know what wheatgrass is, but are consuming it and having amazing sex because of it. Your friends own cars that start with a push of a button. Your friends wash their jeans. Your friends smile because they are happy, because they have nothing to hide, because life is so fucking great. Your friends smile because they mean it. Your friends. Your friends are all smiling. Right now. All at once. Always.

Your Wife

hates Benjamin Franklin, takes underwater photography,
held your dying Rhodesian Ridgeback and wept.

Your wife makes apple pancakes every Sunday, doesn't mind
that you're out late, is staying home with your sick daughter.

Your wife actually pronounces her name quite differently
than what I am saying, doesn't like all this noise,

isn't really your wife but that's what you call her.
Your wife is now your ex-wife, is now your first wife,

is now your late wife. Your wife is a wildcat in bed,
is the only one you ever want to make love to, is struggling

to explain to your therapist exactly what is wrong.
Your wife is on the other side of you, farthest

from the aisle, is unaware that we are having this lunch,
doesn't exist yet but is still a better option than me.

Your wife looks beautiful in white, is the reason
you stopped drinking, is Skyping from Sweden

lifting a champagne glass in the air. Your wife is a person
I've never met, is the picture framed in your office,

was your wife from the moment you saw her,
before she even had a chance to say *hello*.

Married Men

are married. You know this. You were at their wedding. What they say
should land as if your dad said it, or your brother. None of it means harm:
the way you look in a pair of jeans, how long your lipstick lasts, how good
the oysters are, how fresh. Married men are the lead characters in the movie
of their marriage. They share top billing but have earned their solo screen time.
They want you to see how they are without their wives: the same or different?
Married men lean forward when they smile and lean back when they laugh.
After the party, they roam the kitchen, offer to share with you a plate
of reheated hors d'oevres. You see it: still life of some other woman's man,
barefoot & drunk, hungry & alone. You're always sure to keep your distance,
but you still laugh at their terrible jokes. The cat hisses at him. It's his wife's cat.
It hates him, and for the life of him, he can't figure out why.

SELF PORTRAIT AS MY DACHSHUND MAX

Sometimes I try to make eye contact with my dog
and fail. They say it's because he's a rescue, and
that dogs consider eye contact aggressive. I stare

at my dog's small brown face and call him *sweetie*
and *honey* and *baby boy*. His eyebrows flex and quiver.
His pupils volley from one side to the other, but never

look at me. When I reach to touch him he squeezes
his eyes shut. Advice is mixed on whether I should
pet him at this point. I usually do. *Baby. Angel.*

I can never tell if he likes it. When he first arrived,
he hid behind my curtains. He refused water. He panted
and shook. His body was a chorus of pink bald patches.

Stress can do that sometimes, the rescue said, telling me
how he was handed over to them without even a name.
Months later, we are sitting together on the couch

when I notice his eyelashes, how they've started to grow
back, how when he sleeps, they jump and twitch, flutter
like the wings of a small bird preparing to fly.

VI

Not Doing Something Wrong Isn't the Same As Doing Something Right

In my defense, my forgotten breasts. In my defense, the hair
no one brushed from my face. In my defense, my hips.

Months earlier, I remember thinking that sex was a ship retreating
on the horizon. I could do nothing but shove my feet in the sand.

I missed all the things loneliness taught me: eyes that follow you
crossing a room, hands that find their home on you. To be noticed, even.

In my defense, his hands. In my defense, his arms. In my defense,
how when we just sat listening to each other breathe, he said, *This is enough.*

My body was a house I had closed for the winter. It shouldn't have been
that difficult, empty as it was. Still, I stared hard as I snapped off the lights.

My body was a specter that haunted me, appearing when I stripped
in the bathroom, when I crawled into empty beds, when it rained.

My body was abandoned construction, restoration scaffolding
that became permanent. My body's unfinished became its finished.

So in my defense, when he touched me, the lights of my body came on.
In my defense, the windows were thrown open. In my defense, *spring.*

New Year's Eve

You arrived on my doorstep like an unscratched lottery ticket,
ignoring every snuffed light. When I opened the door,
your mouth flashed like a tangled string of Christmas lights.
I remember you easing your shoulders into the frame, waiting.
I remember my small hands, how they palmed both sides of the door.

FEBRUARY

After I drank coffee and you drank wine,
and the beautiful waitress left without giving
us forks so we ate the cake with our fingers;

after winter threw a glass of ice in our faces,
and we pulled our coats tight against our bodies
and let the wind push us into each other on the street;

after the lobby doors gasped when we opened them,
after the heat tumbled into us, and no one heard us
moan from relief; after the elevator door closed,

and we leaned into separate corners, pink-cheeked,
the numbers ticking higher and higher and higher;
after you slid the key in and turned it, and I followed

you into your quiet apartment; after we stripped
off our coats both too fast and too slow, it was then
that I saw your bed, neatly made in the next room.

It was then that the present became the present,
became every possibility, became anything I wanted,
became a room full of hands waiting to feel something.

March

Sometimes I imagine it: I am pressed against a wall,
and it is your new hands holding up my soft neck,
as it would a flower's broken stem. See how my body
collapses towards you, a precise angle of fresh want?

Other times, I imagine we discover each other
in the thick shadows behind your house.
Notice how they hide from the streetlamps,
how they wait for us to be stepped into them?

I wonder if it could ever be that simple, to just walk
into the darkness together. In the morning,
when I brush my teeth, my tongue already wants
to say your name. When did I become this woman

who ignores everything but my body's hot strum?
Whose hands have become ghosts haunting my skin,
restless and searching: for their home, for you,
for that last time they felt alive.

CRUSH

Last night I dreamt that I called my best friend
and told her, *I am doing a bad thing here.*

When I woke up, I was relieved, happy
I hadn't actually done anything wrong.

You can't control your feelings, my therapist friend
once told me, *but you sure as hell can control*

the actions those feelings are trying to provoke.
My brain knows things my heart does not:

You are not the getaway car.
You are not the softest bed.

You are not the answer sheet.
You are not the heavy jacket.

You are not the door prize I get to win
for the Most Busted-Up Heart.

You are not my next morning
so you can't be the night before.

You are not any metaphor
that can work.

So I have to let you go, have my thoughts
be about anything else:

the thick oatmeal of regret I still eat
for breakfast; the sputtering writing

which coughs from my engine;
the mirror I can't stop looking at,

so desperate I am
to see something else.

JULY

The figs we ate wrapped in bacon.
The gelato we consumed greedily:
coconut milk, clove, fresh ginger.
How we'd dump hot espresso on it
just to watch it melt, licking our spoons
clean. The potatoes fried in duck fat,
the salt we'd suck off our fingers,
the eggs we'd watch get beaten
'til they were a dizzying bright yellow,
how their edges crisped in the pan.
The pink salt blossom of prosciutto
we pulled apart with our hands, melted
on our eager tongues. The green herbs
with goat cheese, the aged brie paired
with a small pot of strawberry jam,
the final sour cherry we kept politely
pushing onto each other's plate, saying,
No, you. But it's so good. No, it's yours.
How I finally put an end to it, plucked it
from the plate, and stuck it in my mouth.
How good it tasted: so sweet and so tart.
How good it felt: to want something and
pretend you don't, and to get it anyway.

OCTOBER

More beautiful women have loved you,
more talented. Poems about you have
already been written by better hands.
I can't help but cover up my bare skin.
I flee. I'm not still enough for your love.
My lips are attached to a nervous face.
My *No* is always quicker than my *Yes*.
I want to touch you so badly I don't
know how to even reach out. I'll never
know how to say it: how sunk I am
in this love for you, how salty,
how sweet.

November

Back row of the theater, and I held my bare ankle
like a guard rail, to steady myself. Your hands,
unlit matches in the dark. My throat was so bare,
the air conditioning was a hurricane of feathers.
Its hands were everywhere your mouth was not.

I didn't know there was this want in me:
the outline of your knuckles in the silver light,
your thick wrist, the swell of your forearm,
all the effortless heat you shed. I didn't know
that the desire would break through me,

wave after wave of it, pounding and sudden.
How I worried that you'd turn to see it, that
I wanted to have you pin me in the dark, to be
held down by you, to have all this hunger rise
to my surface and to have you taste it.

Atlas

I didn't smash my home to rubble
to make gravel for this road we're on.

I didn't rip my life all in half, relinquish
all those dreams, cut off my limb

just so I'd have something to light
for a signal flare. And yet,

your chest is becoming the field I want
to be buried in. Your laugh, your hair,

your warm hand surprising the small
of my back as we walk through a door.

The timing, I told you, *the timing*.
When I staggered onto the path

that lead me away from everything I knew,
how could I have possibly known

it was leading me
to you.

Number One With a Bullet

How the sound of you unbuckling
your belt became my favorite song.

How I couldn't get it out of my head,
sung it face down into my pillow.

How I would wait all night,
just to hear you perform it live.

How when you finally did,
my whole body sprung into dance.

In the Dark, He Whispered

If you want it, say it.
If you want it, say MORE.

In the dark, I did not say: *MORE.*
In the dark, I told him: *ALL OF IT.*

After that, he whispered: *Good answer.*
After that, there were no other words to say.

BLUEGRASS

My body is not a tuning fork, but your mouth
still coaxes impossible music from it, throaty
and low. You tell me how beautiful they are,
these songs you pull from me. Tell me how
beautiful the instrument, this body that turns
and turns for you in the night. And I marvel
at how quiet you are, how warm and there:
your face, a night sky I sit beneath in rapture.

December

When my body had forgotten its purpose,
when it just hung off my brainstem like a whipped mule.
When my hands only wrote. When my teeth only ate.
When my ass sat, my eyes read, when my reflexes
were answers to questions we all already knew.
Remember how it was then that you slid your hand
into me, a fork in the electric toaster of my body. Jesus,
where did all these sparks come from? Where was all
this heat? Remember what this mouth did last night?
And still, this morning I answer the phone like normal,
still I drink an hour's worth of strong coffee. And now
I file. And now I send an email. And remember how
my lungs filled with all that everything? Remember
how my heart was an animal you released from its cage?
Remember how we unhinged? Remember all the names
our bodies called each other? Remember how afterwards,
the steam rose from us like a pair of smiling ghosts?

January

It was the year of the unannounced arrival.
The year my fingers felt made to drag tracks
through your hair, to brush beneath your collar,
gentle as an eyelash. The year I'd wait all night
for your hands to trace the length of my shoulders
as we hugged goodbye. The year of the dog walk,
the milkshake, the long shower. The year I'd ride
my bike all day going nowhere. It was the year
of the broken seatbelt, the lock that just wouldn't
click. It was the year of the reckless passenger.
The year you surprised me by opening my door.
The year I found you waiting in the darkened frame
of my door. The year you walked through the open mouth
of my door. It was the year you said, *I remember.*
The year you said, *I always remember when a girl
says she likes something.* It was the year I became
that girl.

MIXED METAPHOR

Remember how I wrote
you were not a getaway car?

Thank you for letting me
ride you hard anyway.

VII

THE CLOSURE HOTEL

I checked in with a suitcase containing every photo
I own of him. Even the one where it's just his hair,
even the ones of just his family. All of them.

I unpacked a menu from every place we've ever eaten.
As I tore each one in half, the restaurants evaporated
from their addresses. The food they served disappeared

from my memory. Soon I'd never eaten a beignet,
never put queso blanco on corn on the cob. Soon,
whole streets were just streets again. At this hotel,

the beds are small, made for one. The pillows are clean,
scentless. Here, my eyes can push out a river of salt. Here,
I can sleep as late as I want, and still, when I wake up,

it's a new morning. There are no calendars, no clocks.
Once I stayed for a whole year and no one said a thing.
The woman at the desk looks like me. She understands,

smiled kindly when I appeared in her lobby last night,
shaking like an ice machine, the smell of his soap
trailing me like a sweet, insistent phantom.

INVENTORY

The way I laughed: too loud and at my own jokes.
The way I never washed my hair. The way I pushed
my food onto my fork with my fingers, just like a lady
wouldn't. How I loved you, stupidly, despite every signal.

How your lips looked. How your hands were so large
and empty. How the hair on your neck let me touch it
sometimes. How you would laugh, despite yourself.
And I'd throw my whole body to the ground to catch it.

How I laughed: loud and sudden, a firecracker startling
your terrier of a heart. How I laughed at everything:
the waitresses, the weather, the way dogs walk so certain
of their happiness. How I laughed even when it hurt,

even when it wasn't funny.

TOURIST IN THE PLACE I USED TO LIVE

New York City is crashing all around me:
the smiling dogs, the women in their sundresses,
the sheepish drivers apologizing through the windshield.
This city is wearing summer well. And I wear it poorly.
I still unpack my swagger when I need to, which isn't
high-end. Poor people swagger is mostly a furrowed
brow and a determined step. Don't fuck with me is
the make-up that ties it all together. I remember when
summer would hold my face against the pavement,
make me say uncle. I remember the sky looking thick
and hopeless, the subway feeling like an angry mother.
I remember wanting to escape and to stay. I escaped.
Now I return an ugly cousin. My plain suitcase and
canvas shoes. My piss-poor attitude. The city smiles
politely at me and touches my heart's cowlick. It says
it admires it. It doesn't even try to flatten it down.

After the Break-Up, a Married Friend Tells Me She's Jealous Because of How Boring Her Marriage Can Be

How you knew how to hold me when we slept, arms looped
around my shoulders, one leg draped over my hip. How I'd
roll into you in the night and you'd turn to hold me, instinct,
as if you were made to do it. The happy groan we'd share.

The fries we would eat off each other's plates, the waiters
who greeted us by name, how when we got sick, we knew
exactly the brand of soda, the movie to put on, the blanket
to drag out. How you'd put socks on my cold feet.

Even now, there are so many streets in so many cities
where I remember holding your hand, meals we ate,
our laughing eyes. You are still *everywhere*. Even now,
I remember how happy we were, how simple it was.

Tell me how do you undo these years of bone knowledge,
these ways I loved you without even knowing it?

THE END OF IT

I.
To end doesn't mean that something is a failure,
a character in a movie once told me: *Everyone ceases
to exist. It doesn't mean everyone's a failure.*

And I tell this to people all the time to explain us,
our slow unraveling, how our great love dissolved
to white, and in its place, this new thing: *friendship.*

Because our romance ended doesn't mean it failed,
I say, it was a great success. We loved so much, so hard,
so long. We loved until we couldn't love anymore.

II.
When you and I talk now,
I flood with joyful relief:

the engine of my love still
running under this new hood;

the trunk of this new friendship
holding so much.

III.
When are you going to get angry? a divorcing friend asks.
Never? I answer. *He is not a bad person for not being
in love with me anymore.* To say it out loud. To mean it.
To know it, true as a toothache. To remember how badly
I wanted to have it back, your love. How hard I fought.
But in the end, how even I knew. Like how trees know
to let go of their leaves, that nothing can stop the winter.

IV.
When someone asks after you now,
their faces are a slow motion flinch.
They love you so much, they can't help
but worry a dark cloud.

When someone asks about me now,
their faces are my high school guidance counselor,
so sure everything will work out they never actually
look at me.

V.
Details aren't important, no matter
who asks. What, or how, or why.
It's whether we stick the landing.
To me, the ending is all that matters.
And old love, we made it. We are
on the other side. We are okay.

VI.
We did not become villains.
We did not become martyrs.
We did not become broken.
We did not become strangers
We became different.
We became *friends*.
We became a pair of boots
which at first blistered us to blood,
but that we can now pull on easy,
everyday, worn and comfortable,
knowing we can walk through anything.

VII.
In the end, know this: I regret nothing.
Not the beginning. Not the finish.
Not any moment in between.

All the poems, all the photos, every kiss
I demanded from you in the kitchen. Every drop
we collected in our bucket hearts.

VIII.
New York City feels like a dream now,
you once told me, and I understood exactly
what you meant. Yesterday I was given

a photograph of us in our first year. My hand
on your cheek, your happy paw on my waist.
We didn't know the picture was being taken.

Our faces were two bright suns shining only
for each other. *My God,* I couldn't help but
think, *I wonder if I will ever be in love like that.*

Acknowledgements

Grateful thankful are given to the following organizations whose support were absolutely instrumental in the creation of this book:

the **National Endowment for Arts** for granting me a 2011 NEA Literature Fellowship in Poetry;

the **University of Pennsylvania** and the **Kelly Writers House** for naming me their 2010-2011 ArtsEdge Writer-in-Residence;

and the **Berkshire Taconic Community Foundation** for naming me their 2013 Amy Clampitt House Writer-in-Residence.

Grateful acknowledgements also are made to the following literary journals, in which some of these writings first appeared in slightly different forms:

Amethyst Arsenic – "The Road Most Travelled Never Left Queens"
Bakery – "Not Doing Something Wrong Isn't The Same As Doing Something Right" and "Wild Geese"
Brusque – "Trickle Down Economics"
CAP Magazine – "Self Portrait as My Dachshund Max"
Criminal Class Review – "Every Bad Thought"
Danse Macabre – "A Brief History of the Bowery Poetry Club," "In the Dark, He Whispered" and "Unemployment"
decomP – "Orange Socks"
Dirtcakes – "The Waiting Room of the GYN" and "Right There Yes"
Dressing Room Poetry Journal – "The Telling"
Foxing Quarterly – "Number One With a Bullet"
Frigg – "November," "July" and "February"
Gulf Coast – "Your Wife"
iO: A Journal of New American Poetry: "Married Men" and "Triptych: August 2011"
kill author – "Brooklyn," "West Philadelphia" and "Austin"
Muzzle – "December"
Negative Suck – "The Bowery"
Orange Room Review – "June"
PANK (print) – "My Tiny God"

PANK (online) – "New Year's Eve"
Post Road Magazine – "What I Meant When I Said Failure" and "Through the Looking Glass"
Rattle – "Op-Ed for The Sad Sack Review" and "Things That Happened During Petsitting That I Remind Myself Are Not Metaphors For My Heart"
Slab – "Bowery Bees"
Some Weird Sin – "Summer Weather" "Mixed Metaphor" and "How We Do"
Subterranean Quarterly – "What Could Go Wrong"
The Legendary – "On Walking In New York City," "Crush," "March" and "October"
The New – "33 & 1/3"
Radius – "Simulacrum"
Thrush – "An Unintentional Metaphor For What Happened Next," "Inventory" "These United States" and "January"
Treehouse – "Said the Fly Killing Itself Trying to Escape thru a Closed Window, Completely Ignoring the Open Door"
Union Station Magazine – "The Poets Wedding in New Orleans"
Used Furniture Review – "Horrible Moving Tips You Could Glean from My Most Recent Move," "Shortly After Moving to Philadelphia for a Writing Residency, I Decide to Walk Home in a Goddamn Heat Wave" and "The End of It"

And lastly, special thanks to **Wess Mongo Jolley** from the IndieFeed Performance Poetry Podcast Channel (performancepoetry. indiefeeed.com) and **Jeffrey Kay** from the SpeakEasyNYC YouTube channel (http://www.youtube.com/user/speakeasynyc) for showcasing so many these poems in audio and video formats.

About the Author

CRISTIN O'KEEFE APTOWICZ is the author of five previous books of poetry— *Dear Future Boyfriend, Hot Teen Slut, Working Class Represent, Oh Terrible Youth* and *Everything is Everything*—which are all currently available through Write Bloody Publishing. She is also the author of the nonfiction book, *Words In Your Face: A Guided Tour Through Twenty Years of the New York City Poetry Slam* (Soft Skull Press), which Billy Collins wrote "leaves no doubt that the slam poetry scene has achieved legitimacy and taken its rightful place on the map of contemporary literature." Her most recent awards include the 2010-2011 ArtsEdge Writer-In-Residency at the University of Pennsylvania, a 2011 National Endowment for the Arts Fellowship in Poetry and the 2013 Amy Clampitt House Residency. Her second book of nonfiction, *Curiosity: Thomas Dent Mütter and the Dawn of Modern Medicine*, will be released by Gotham Books (Penguin) in Fall 2014. She lives in Austin, TX, with two eccentric rescue dachshunds.

For more information, including upcoming tour dates, please visit her website at:

www.aptowicz.com

IF YOU LIKE CRISTIN O'KEEFE APTOWICZ, CRISTIN O'KEEFE APTOWICZ LIKES...

I Love Science!
Shanny Jean Maney

Rise of the Trust Fall
Mindy Nettifee

The New Clean
Jon Sands

Ceremony for the Choking Ghost
Karen Finneyfrock

No Matter the Wreckage
Sarah Kay

Write Bloody Publishing distributes and promotes great books of fiction, poetry and art every year. We are an independent press dedicated to quality literature and book design, with an office in Austin, TX.

Our employees are authors and artists so we call ourselves a family. Our design team comes from all over America: modern painters, photographers and rock album designers create book covers we're proud to be judged by.

We publish and promote 8-12 tour-savvy authors per year. We are grass-roots, D.I.Y., bootstrap believers. Pull up a good book and join the family. Support independent authors, artists and presses.

Want to know more about Write Bloody books, authors and events?
Join our maling list at

www.writebloody.com

IF YOU LIKE *THE YEAR OF NO MISTAKES*, CHECK OUT CRISTIN'S OTHER BOOKS...

Dear Future Boyfriend
In her quirky debut volume, Cristin O'Keefe Aptowicz tackles love ("Science"), heartbreak ("Lit") and thieving suburban punks ("Ode to the Person Who Stole My Family's Lawn Gnome"), among other hilariously idiosyncratic topics.

Hot Teen Slut
In her second collection of poetry, Cristin O'Keefe Aptowicz serves up a memoir-in-verse her first job out of college: writing and editing for porn. Aptowicz dramatizes the hopes, humor and ambitions of a young poet's first steps into a very surreal "real world."

Working Class Represent
In her third collection of poetry, Cristin O'Keefe Aptowicz celebrates the ups and downs of being performance poet with a day job. This book continues Aptowicz's tradition of witty, honest and wildly original work.

Oh, Terrible Youth
In her fourth collection of poetry, Cristin O'Keefe Aptowicz uses her youth as muse. This plump collection commiserates and celebrates all the wonder, terror, banality and comedy that is the long journey through to adulthood.

Everything is Everything
In her fifth collection of poetry, Cristin O'Keefe Aptowicz polishes her obsessions until they gleam. *Everything is Everything* illuminates the dark corners of the curiosity cabinet, shining the light on everything that is utterly strange, wonderfully absurd and 100% true.

ALL BOOKS ARE AVAILABLE
ON WRITE BLOODY PUBLISHING

America's Independent Press

WRITE BLOODY BOOKS

After the Witch Hunt — Megan Falley

Aim for the Head, Zombie Anthology — Rob Sturma, Editor

Amulet — Jason Bayani

Any Psalm You Want — Khary Jackson

Birthday Girl with Possum — Brendan Constantine

The Bones Below — Sierra DeMulder

Born in the Year of the Butterfly Knife — Derrick C. Brown

Bring Down the Chandeliers — Tara Hardy

Ceremony for the Choking Ghost — Karen Finneyfrock

Courage: Daring Poems for Gutsy Girls — Karen Finneyfrock, Mindy Nettifee
& Rachel McKibbens, Editors

Dear Future Boyfriend — Cristin O'Keefe Aptowicz

Dive: The Life And Fight Of Reba Tutt — Hannah Safren

Drunks and Other Poems of Recovery — Jack McCarthy

The Elephant Engine High Dive Revival anthology

Everything is Everything — Cristin O'Keefe Aptowicz

The Feather Room — Anis Mojgani

Gentleman Practice — Buddy Wakefield

Glitter in the Blood: A Guide to Braver Writing — Mindy Nettifee

Good Grief — Stevie Edwards

The Good Things About America — Derrick Brown and Kevin Staniec, Editors

Hot Teen Slut — Cristin O'Keefe Aptowicz

I Love Science! — Shanny Jean Maney

I Love You is Back — Derrick C. Brown

The Importance of Being Ernest — Ernest Cline

In Search of Midnight — Mike McGee

The Incredible Sestina Anthology — Daniel Nester, Editor

Junkyard Ghost Revival anthology

Kissing Oscar Wilde — Jade Sylvan